THE SALT

THE SALT

Peter Schireson

Copyright©2018 Peter Schireson
All Rights Reserved
Published by Unsolicited Press
Cover Image: Martinique," by Andre Kertesz
Cover Design: Nate Miller

No part of this book may be reproduced or transmitted in any form or by any means without written permission from the publisher or author.

Printed in the United States of America.

Attention schools and businesses: for discounted copies on large orders, please contact the publisher directly.

ISBN: 978-1-947021-57-0

for my teachers

Contents

Love in the Rainy Season	1
Self-Portrait with Tree	2
Infinity	3
The Salt	4
Proem	7
Divinity	8
Aspiration	9
God of Mildew	10
Violets	13
Fisherman of Dreams	14
Walking	16
Happiness	17
Weeding	18
Double-jointed	19
Shanty	20
Trigger Warnings	21
Memorial	23
Table for Two	24
About the Author	25
Acknowledgements	26

THE SALT

*The doorbell rings...
it would have been
more useful
to cry beforehand.*

Love in the Rainy Season

You brought noodles
Mine was the small cottage in back
You padded around like a documentary
Your short haircut and bony face earnest and
    strong
I, generous with approval
Your pants too short
My perfect little bathroom
Your narrow lips
I served brown bread and cheese
You trimmed my toenails
A bee flew in through a broken window
You cried with laughter
I played the harmonica loud
You smelled of mint
I wondered what would happen

Self-Portrait with Tree

I want to have you,
I murmur
to the photograph in an airport
of a tree on a ridge,
its frail silver gelatin silhouette
leaning against a bright sky.
The shadow hovering
at the edge of the frame
must be me.

Infinity

It has a wish, you said.
When a skirt has a fold like that,
small and unintended in the hem,
it means it has a wish.
I bent over and straightened it,
trying to imagine what more,
beside brushing
against your legs,
sheathed about you, folded,
your pale green skirt
could wish for.

The Salt

I set out to attain nothing more
than myself, and before long,
had no money
and only one tooth,
the price I paid
to locate this exotic kingdom,
where mud-caked holy men
wander barefoot from place
to arduous place,
where the people need salt,
find it in the sea, call
what we call sea, "The Salt,"
and sing, "Let us walk
along the shore of The Salt."
Yes, that will be the title.

Diagnostic

I dreamed I was a poet,
and it was exactly
like being a poet,
except for waking up.

Pilgrim's Progress

On a bright March afternoon, a man strides along a crowded sidewalk—tall, slim, late-60s, thick white hair, and well dressed. I watch him speak to each person he passes, then nod his head as if to agree with himself. A moment later and he and I are face to face. He whispers to me, "I hate you." Do I know this man? Some distant offense? My mind scrambles, then I overhear him speak to the person behind me: "I hate you," and again to the next—cordial and concise. A year goes by. I can't stop thinking about the encounter. "I hate you." I utter the words silently to myself again and again, until finally, I begin to whisper them each time I encounter another person. All my life I've felt I'm climbing a steep hill, lugging a backpack full of rocks. With each "I hate you" I remove a rock. Sidewalk, sunlight, strangers—fresh, pure, exhilarating. And what if that March day I'd walked down a different street, or stopped to look in a window? I would never have known this happiness.

Proem

In a dark bed before the poem,
under each muddle, a muddle:
raw matter, joints in the skeleton,
a deer leaps into the road, the diver
vanishes into the water.
What does it feel like to be a fly?
Because of the eye, the world,
because of world, the I.
I clutch my head and sigh.
Somebody scrape it out, write it down,
all of it, nothing brushed aside,
no one is sleeping,
a night deep in the tarn.

Divinity

The radio preacher explains the Soul Conjecture: how small parts of a geometrical figure can be used to deduce the whole, and that God can be deduced in the same way. The idea drifts through my mind like secondhand smoke, preacher smoke: small parts of God—sparrows on pillars of air, white apricot, pale, lucent skin, yellow blush, rush of sugar, and that curvy plastic thing in the hardware store—what was that thing?

Aspiration

A mosquito just landed on my arm;
one of us
is the footnote.

God of Mildew

Like a caper in an old movie—
piquant, a couple of martinis, a hint of grace—
our conversation snakes through
a disarray of language in the dark restaurant.
Thinking grinds its meanings.
I begin to tell it.

I wake at three a.m. most nights, grumpy, leaden-
eyed, sweat in elbow creases, behind my knees,
around my neck. Sostenuto of tidings from the
body. One night last week, I was hungry for olives.
Eating them, I thought about sunlight
on olive trees, then thought,
It's a mistake to think so much,
just eat the olives. Then I thought, Thinking that
thinking is a mistake might also be
a mistake.

I bought a nightingale. All night
it sang and flew around. Fucking nightingale!

I try to imagine beautiful futures,
old cities in leaf like ancient trees.

I read an article in *Popular Science* about tongue
diagnosis in Chinese medicine. Later, on page two
of *Living and Entertainment,* I saw Miley Cyrus
sticking out her tongue
at the Billboard Music Awards show;

the tip was carmine, a sign
of resentment and depression.

My arrival never greeted me
and my journey doesn't know who I am.
I'm sure I'm on the wrong train,
because I'm on it.

On my fifth birthday, the milkman gave me
a pet duck. It quacked in our yard through one
rainy summer, mysterious as a Vermeer.
A duck's penis is shaped like a corkscrew, and its
love is beguiling, but ultimately unusable.
It disappeared without warning that autumn.

When did everything become so annoying?
Parking spaces at the drug store are too narrow,
and this is not a real bagel.
I have zero interest in returning to Florence
and Mozart is cloying.

My thinking moves
like an old department store elevator, operated by
a young woman named Clarissa, who wears a terse
grey uniform and matching gloves.
She announces the floors and sundry goods
in a clear voice as the elevator descends:
Seven: To-do lists—Bank, Greek yogurt, printer
    paper, Tater Tots.
Six: I promised my wife I would not forget
   to go to the bank, promised and yet,
   again she reminds me, Go to the bank.

Five: Martin's puffy face, Martin who shames me.
　　Why do I continue?
Four: Sexual fantasy—Clarissa.
Three: Ideas for poems: puffy faces, cactus as
　　introvert, brevity is the.
Two: Clarissa in patent leather boots. No, wait: her
　　name is Clarita and she is eating
　　a burrito.
The elevator appears to be stuck.

Violets

In the thick
of our holy quarrel
you leaned in
to whisper
the most important thing,
but were silent,
and I wanted to leave you
alone
across the table
on your device,
but I knocked over our old vase
spilling the violets,
and you looked at me
as if before they fell,
you'd seen them
already fallen.

Fisherman of Dreams

In a King Kong t-shirt
sipping spearmint tea,
I take-up residence
in my mind's watery part
and dream of frolicking
with my fellow apes,
their numberless heads on top of my own.

In the morning, I bathe naked
with the bathroom window open.
Do my neighbors talk about me?
On the porch, I read aloud
from the Vimalakirti Sutra, 32,000 tall,
    spacious, beautiful thrones,
loud enough to be heard across the street.

At work I am promoted to Department
    Manager, give a sparkling PowerPoint,
speech rising like carbonation.
I tilt my head to allow
for the seasons and the tides,
as if my head were Earth itself.

In a congested coffee shop,
walls the white of lipstick favored
by twelve-year-old girls,
my cell phone battery dies
and they run out of apple pie,
so I have peach with ice cream,

a quiet adventure, and I wonder,
could it end right here?

Walking

after a big plate of pork enchiladas,
I farted,
and you replied, "I know."

Happiness

I didn't expect you.
I was just sitting here
watching my mutt, Buster,
twitching in his sleep, and...
What? You're leaving? But
you just got here.

Weeding

Weeding the carnations, you cry.
You say you feel you're vanishing,
that you really do want to vanish before
your gums pull away from your teeth,
and you forget to turn off the stove.
Your mother gave you marked-down bananas
and a washcloth for your birthday,
weeps reading TV Guide aloud,
deploys random nouns—
Burger King, grandchild, teacup, giraffe—as
    adjectives,
roosts in assisted living
on her bed in a posture of conversation,
lips parted, leaning in, but looking away.
"What's it like to be ninety-six, Louise?" I ask.
"Not everything is like something else, dear,"
    she says.
"Don't be Walmart."

Double-jointed

Fall knocked on the sky
like a newspaper flung against the door.
You marched up the stairs,
pearls against a white dress,
in one hand a spray of lavender.
A man whistled in the street below,
the wooden horse neighed in the wind—
called to the meadow,
you went back down.

Shanty

To be the fable waiting for the prince would be delightful, but not the prince waiting for the fable. Otherwise, to be the prince's ship imagining the sea, or the sea envisioning the prince's ship provisioned for the voyage, or to be myself a sailor aboard, pitiless waves spreading further and further away, but not the fog or the ship lost in it, rats deserting, the prince fallen to assassins, the ruptured hull, drowning men in the water. Perhaps just to be a terrace overlooking the sea, awaiting the prince's arrival, ignorant of all the rest, would suit me best.

Trigger Warnings

I believed I knew the contents
of the firing chamber, knew
the sear surface and hammer materials,
    until one day at the zoo,
as I leaned on a railing watching the gibbons
    balletic,
I saw in the acrylic panel enclosing the cage
my own reflection, an unarticulated skeleton in a
specimen jar.
    As snow fell in late afternoon,
and with regard to the color crimson,
I considered how snow and crimson sometimes left
me distressed by the sound
of my own shattery breath,
    how hearing
a guilty verdict on the radio while driving
to my parent's house made me feel
like slapping myself.
    I really can't say
if my index finger is required
to actuate a firing sequence,
or my thumb to activate the cocking machinery,
but while swimming laps at the Y,
the pale skin of the old man in the next lane
wearing a blue bathing cap
provoked an encounter with solitude,
bringing tears that pooled in my goggles.
    On a couch
at the end of the hospital corridor,

watching the night custodian buff the linoleum
aroused a trumpeting angel beast.
    Another evening,
as I urinated in the bathroom of my favorite bar
while they were playing "Rap God," which I love,
I was consumed by loneliness, and then, later,
strange purification.
        I don't know anything
        about the safety or logic
        of the trigger mechanism,
        nor can I say with any certainty
        how easy or difficult to release
        the hammer.

Memorial

I'm coming to the cemetery tonight,
I'm going to lie on top of your grave,
pull a blanket up over us,
and whisper to you as birdsong.
Hu hu hu—
Mottled Owl croons how
I miss your coconut pie for breakfast,
how after all, only you knew
Hannah Jane— that would have been
her name—the child
we decided not to have.

Table for Two

We dreamed of a life of pâté en croute,
always arriving with a fig mostarda,
a life in which a contralto-green cilantro pesto
could be counted on to refresh the gamey lamb.
Why should the search for perfect cheese puffs be
less important than the search
for pure black or the sound of one hand?
Together, we would change the world
one warm French potato salad at a time.

Tonight, the truffles ebony, the marrow gleaming,
your glass eye gazes out across the dining room
from the sepia photo over the bar,
and all these years later, here am I, a man
of a certain age, overcome with nostalgia,
near tears, my carefully mussed hair
glistening in the incandescent light.

About the Author

Peter Schireson began writing after a long career, first in education, then in business. His poems have appeared in *Quiddity, Hotel Amerika, Painted Bride Quarterly*, and *Pleiades*, among many other journals. His chapbook - The *Welter of Me & You* - won the Coal Hill 2013 Chapbook Prize. Peter holds a Doctorate in Education from Harvard University and an MFA from the Program for Writers at Warren Wilson College. He is also an ordained Zen Buddhist priest, having trained in both the U.S. and Japan. Together with his wife, Grace Schireson, he edited *Zen Bridge: The Zen Teachings of Keido Fukushima*.

Acknowledgements

Thanks to the following journals for publishing versions of these poems:

Arts & Letters, "Trigger Warnings"
Construction Magazine, "The Salt"
Hotel Amerika, "Self-Portrait with Tree"
Painted Bride, "Walking"
The American Journal of Poetry, "God of Mildew"
The Café Review, "Memorial"
The Tampa Review, "Weeding"